24
Stunning
Grayscale Images

COLORING BOOKS

THIS BOOK BELONGS TO

ALENA

ALENA

Published by CreateSpace Independent Publishing Platform

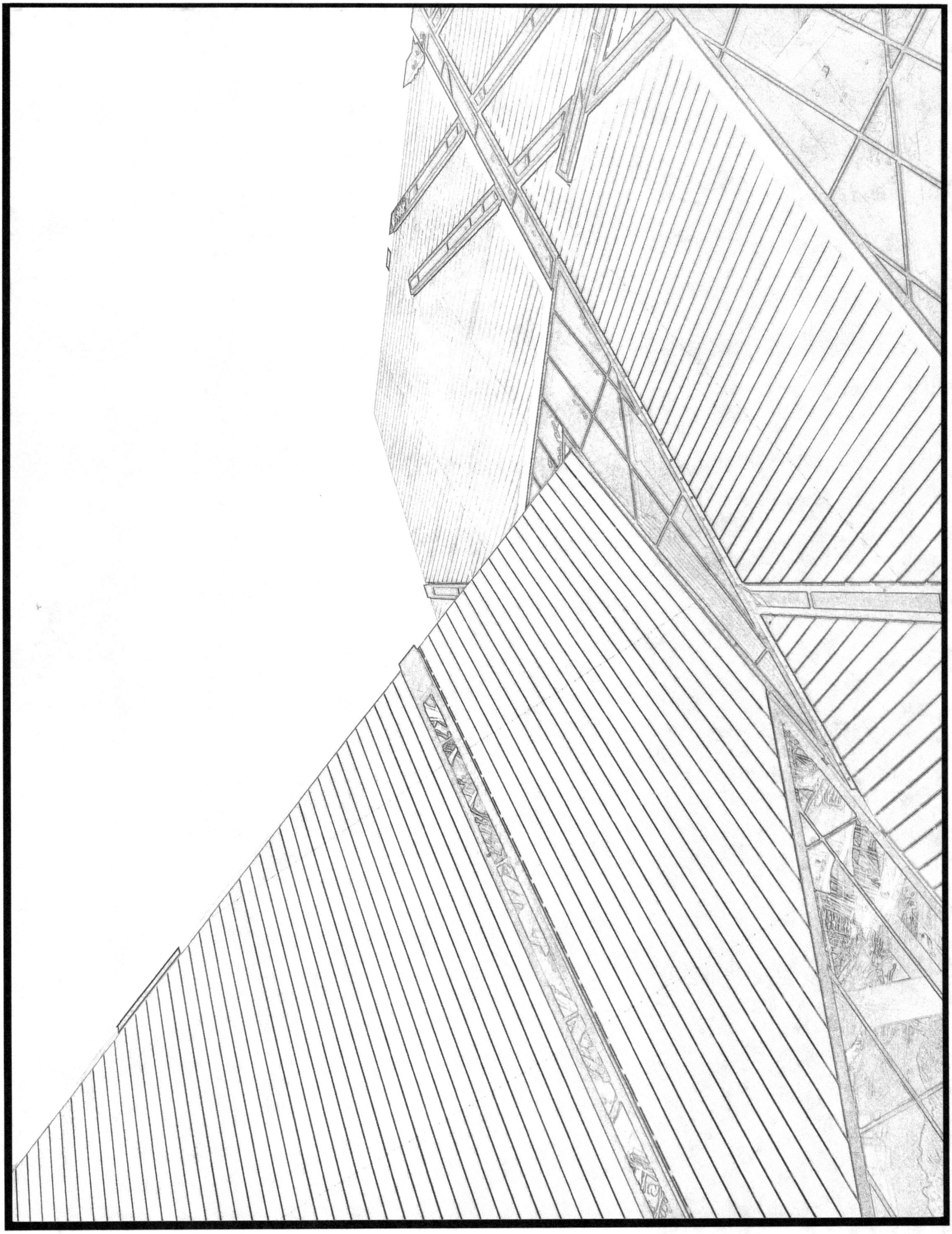

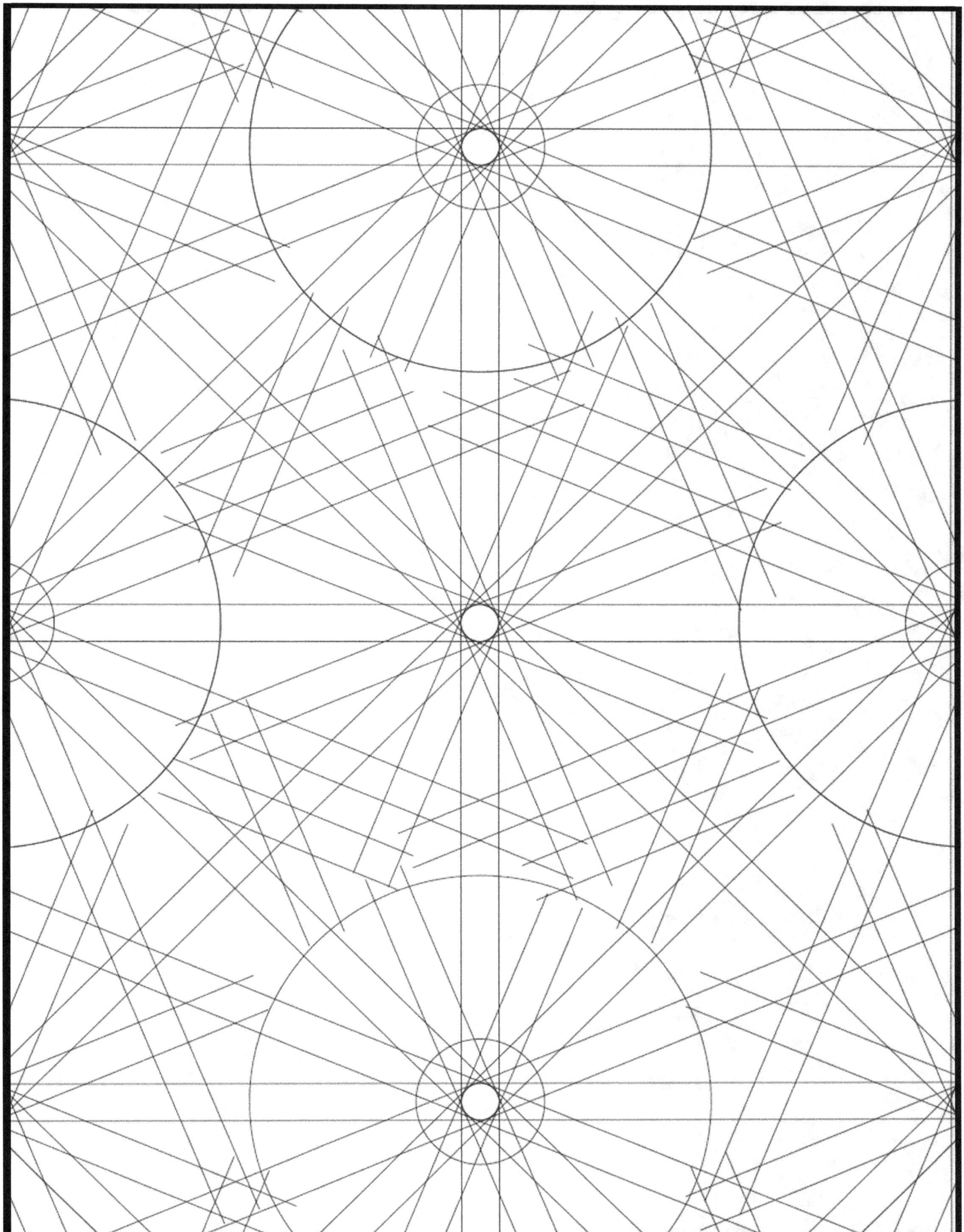

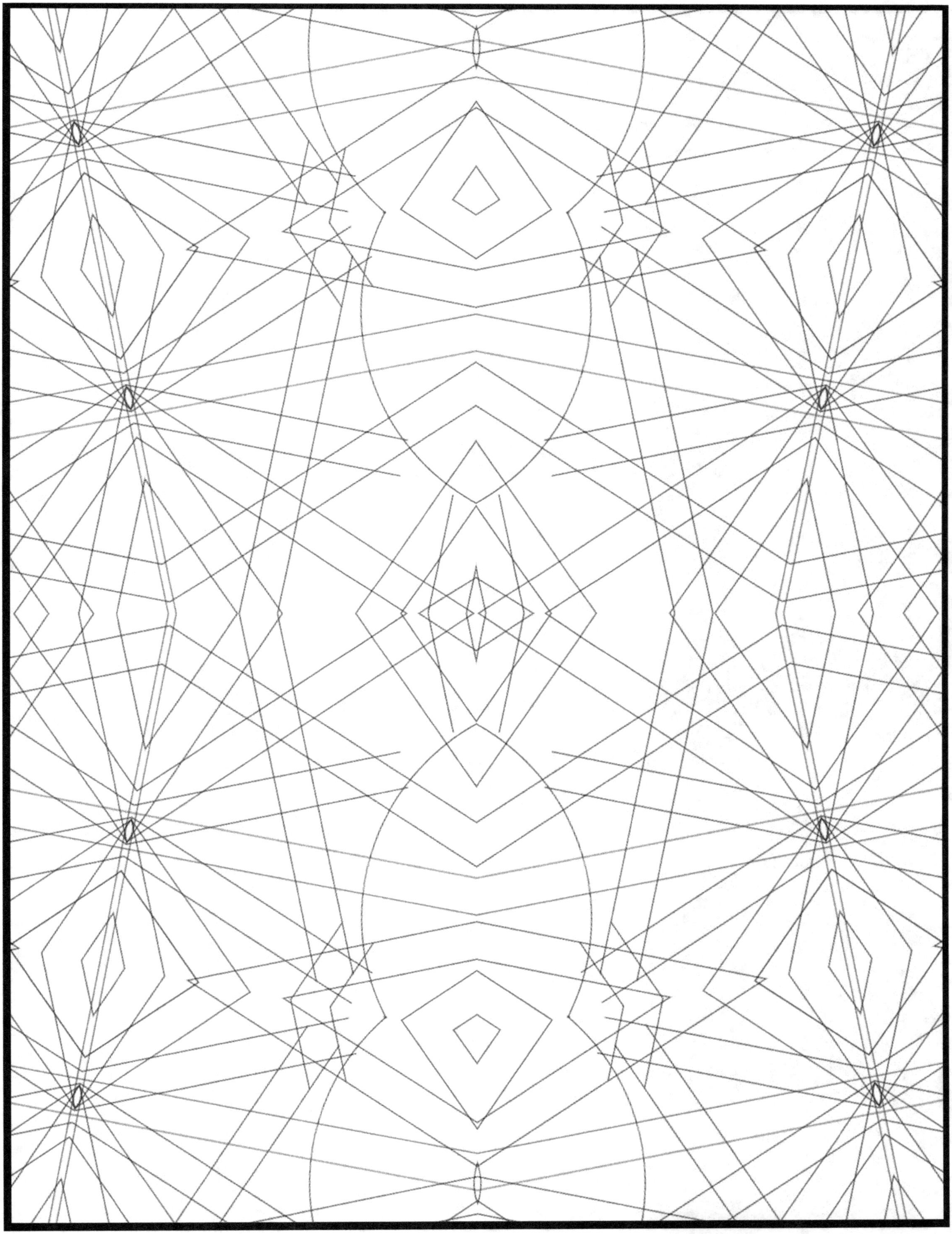

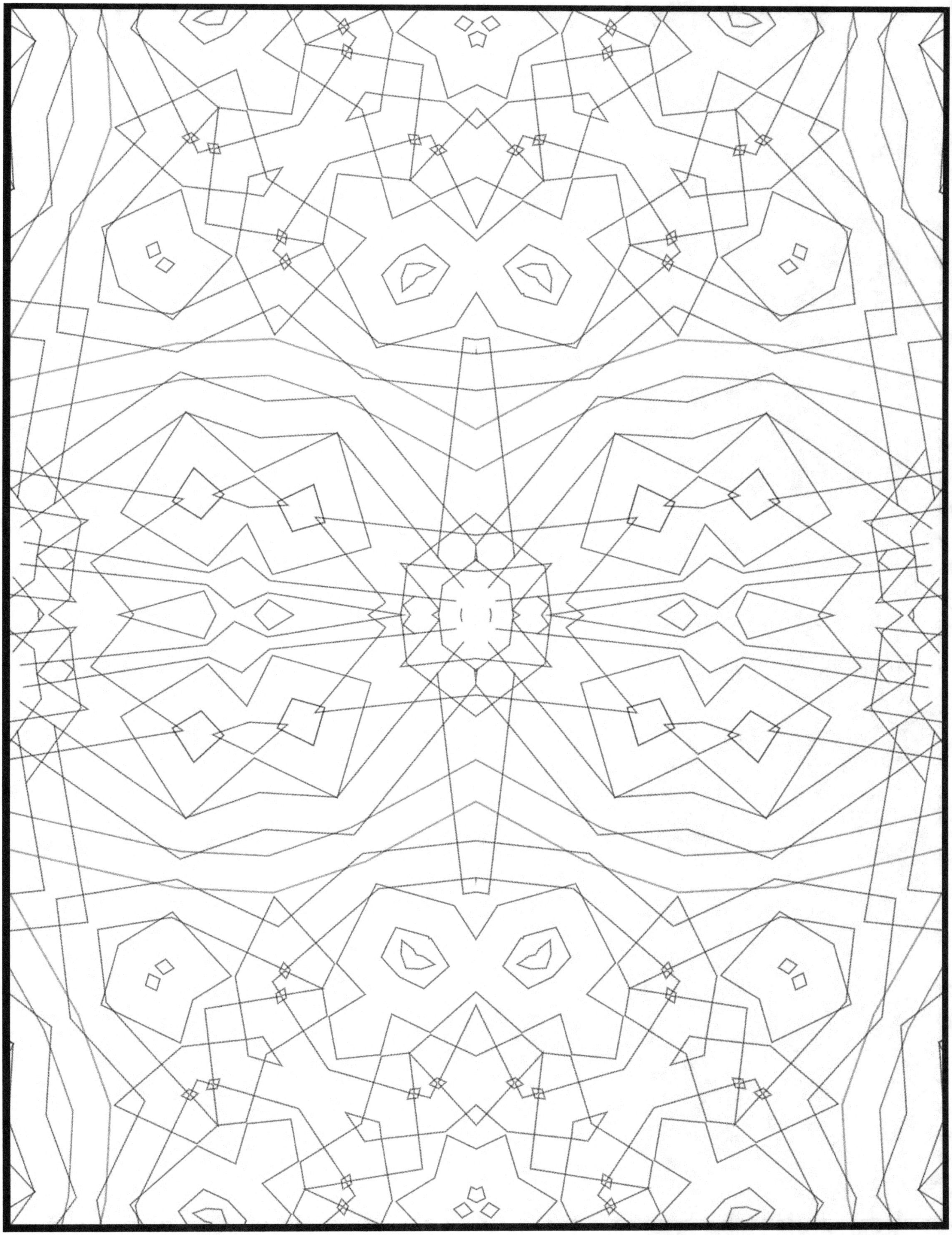

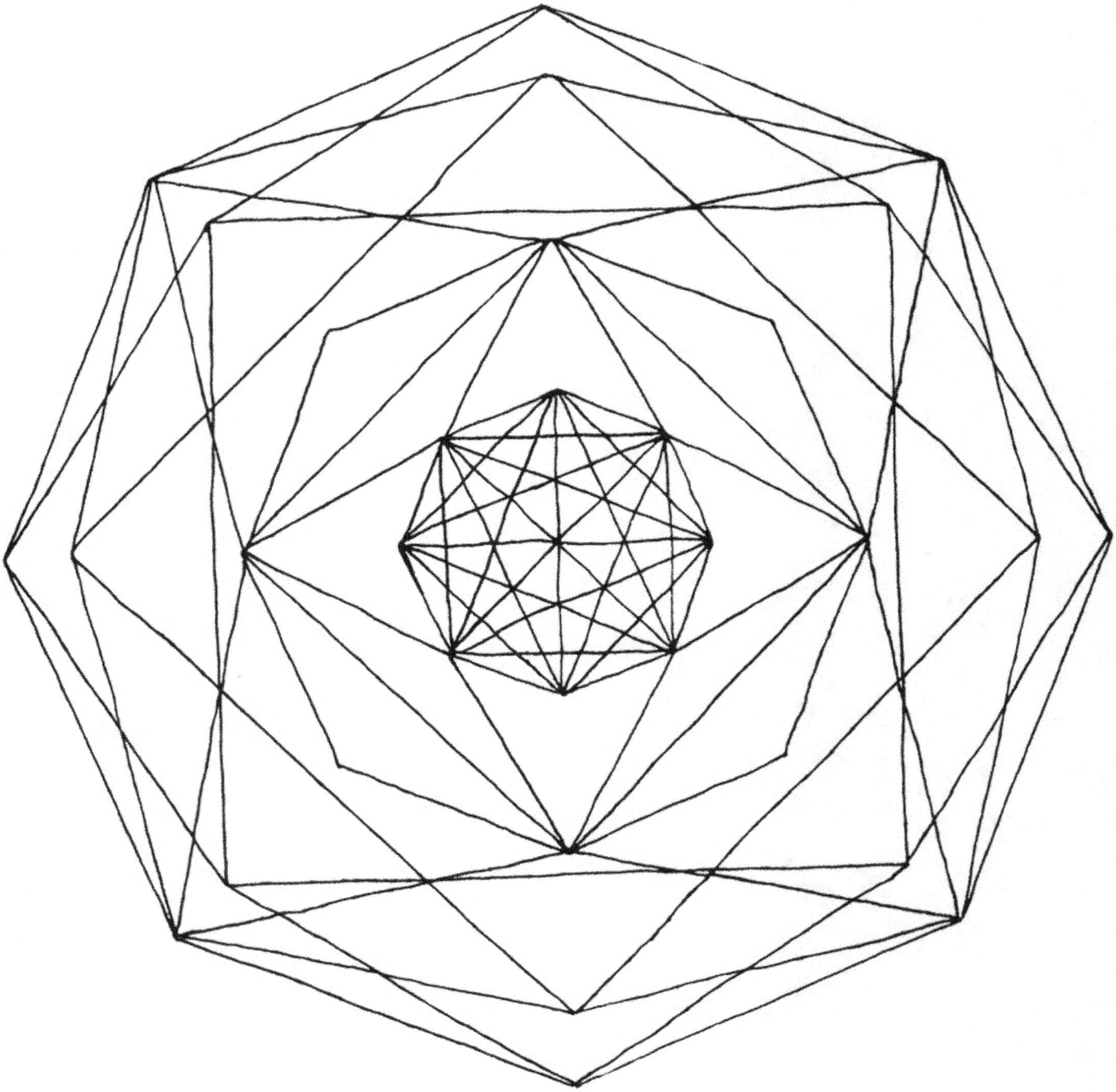

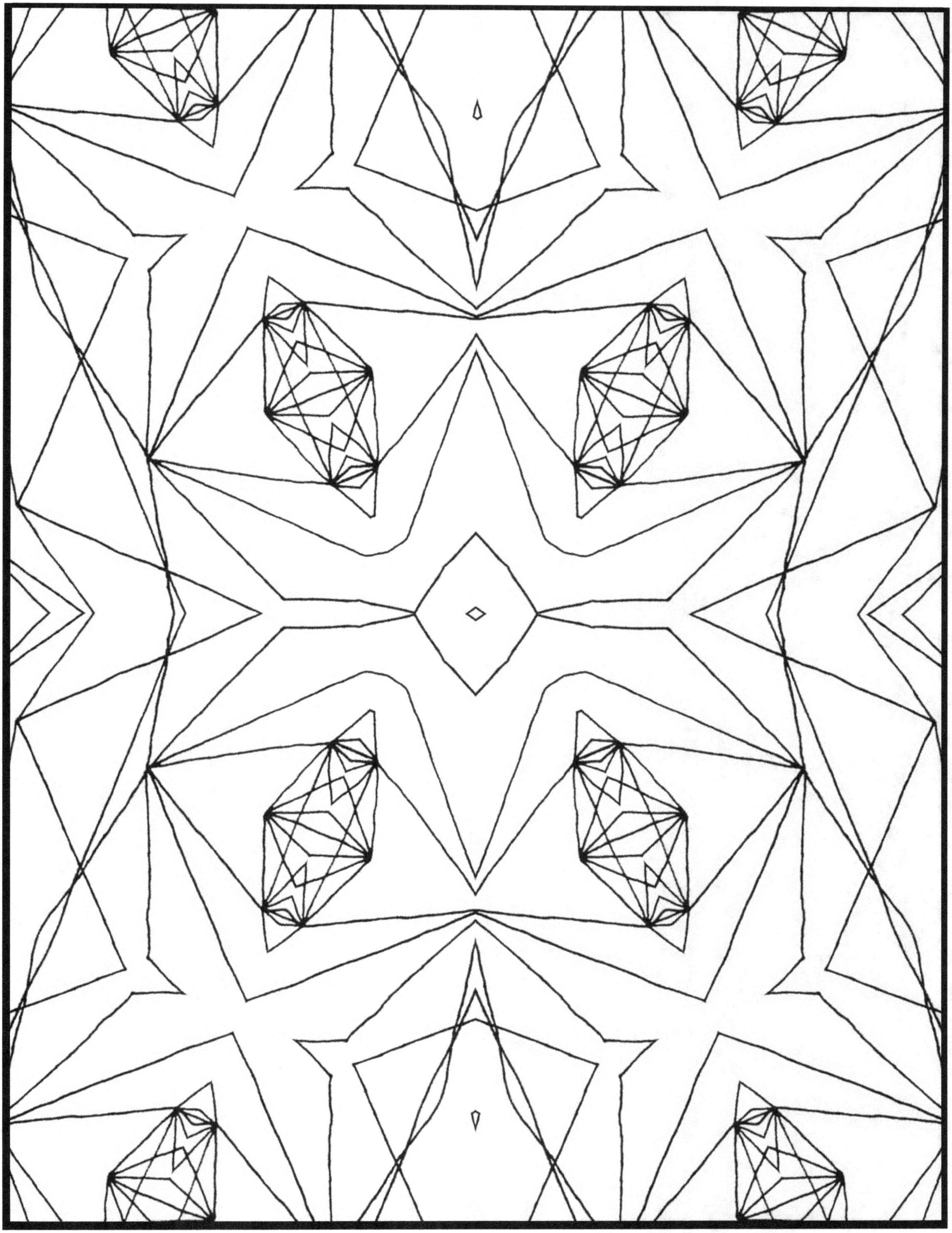

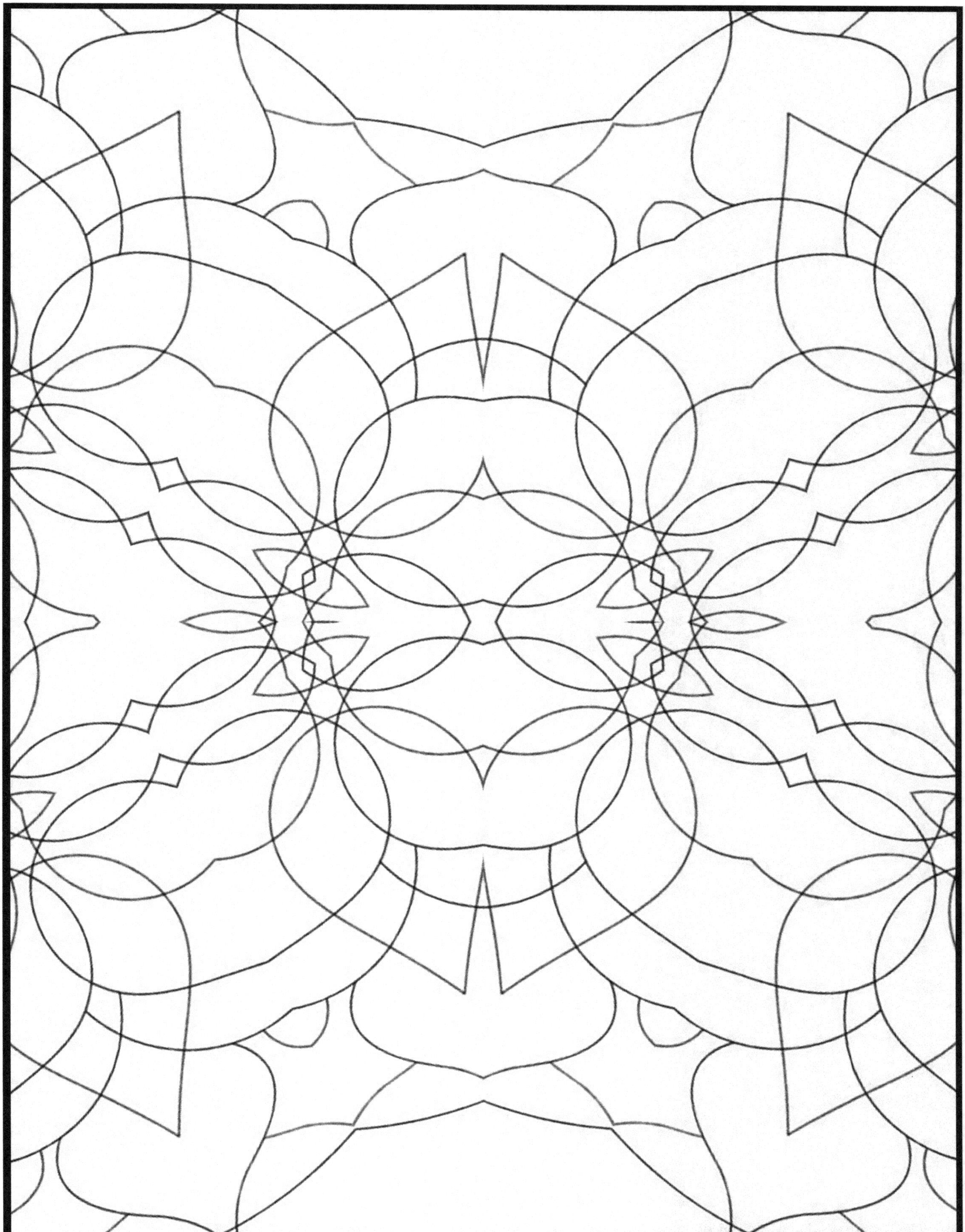

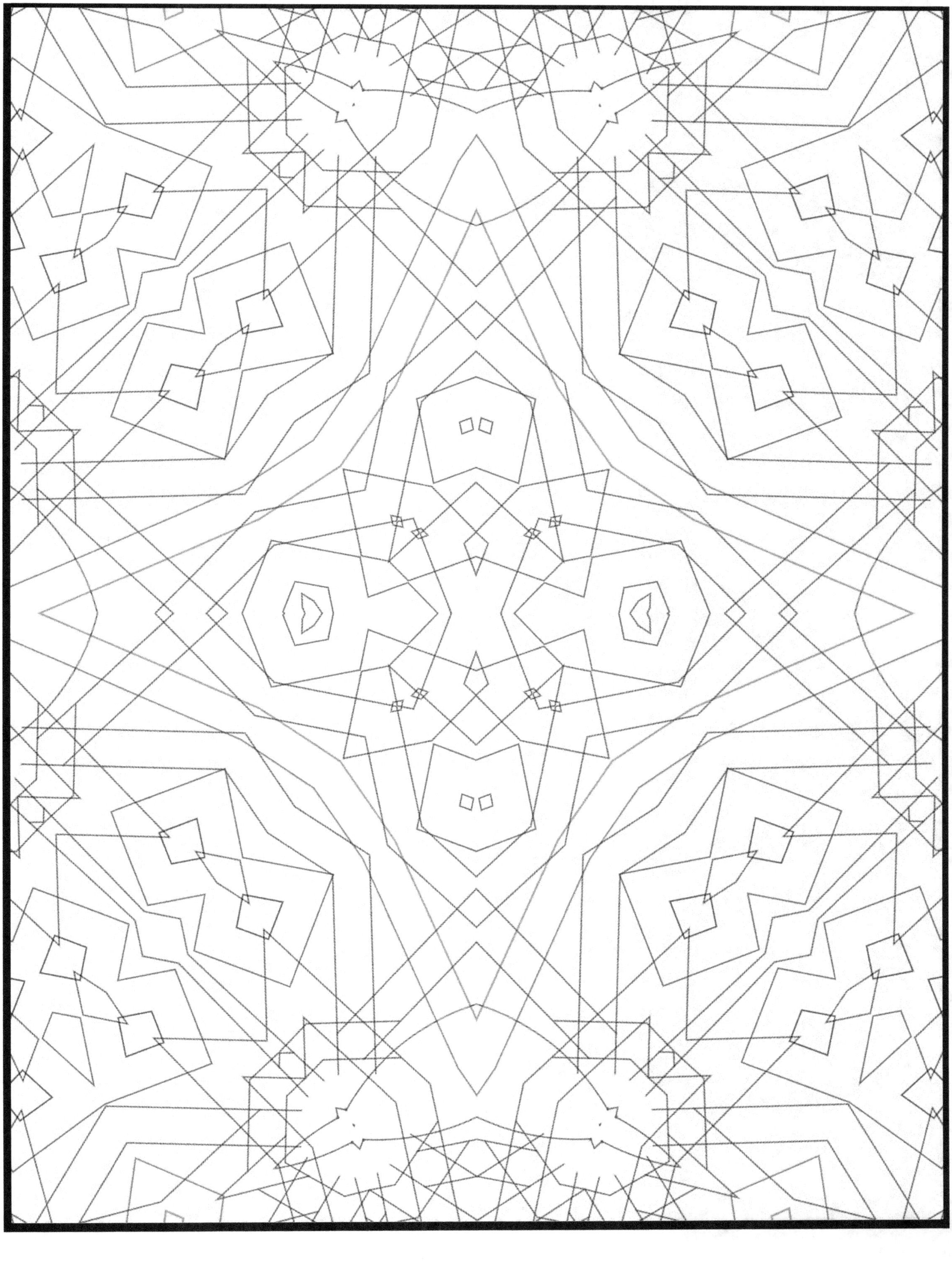

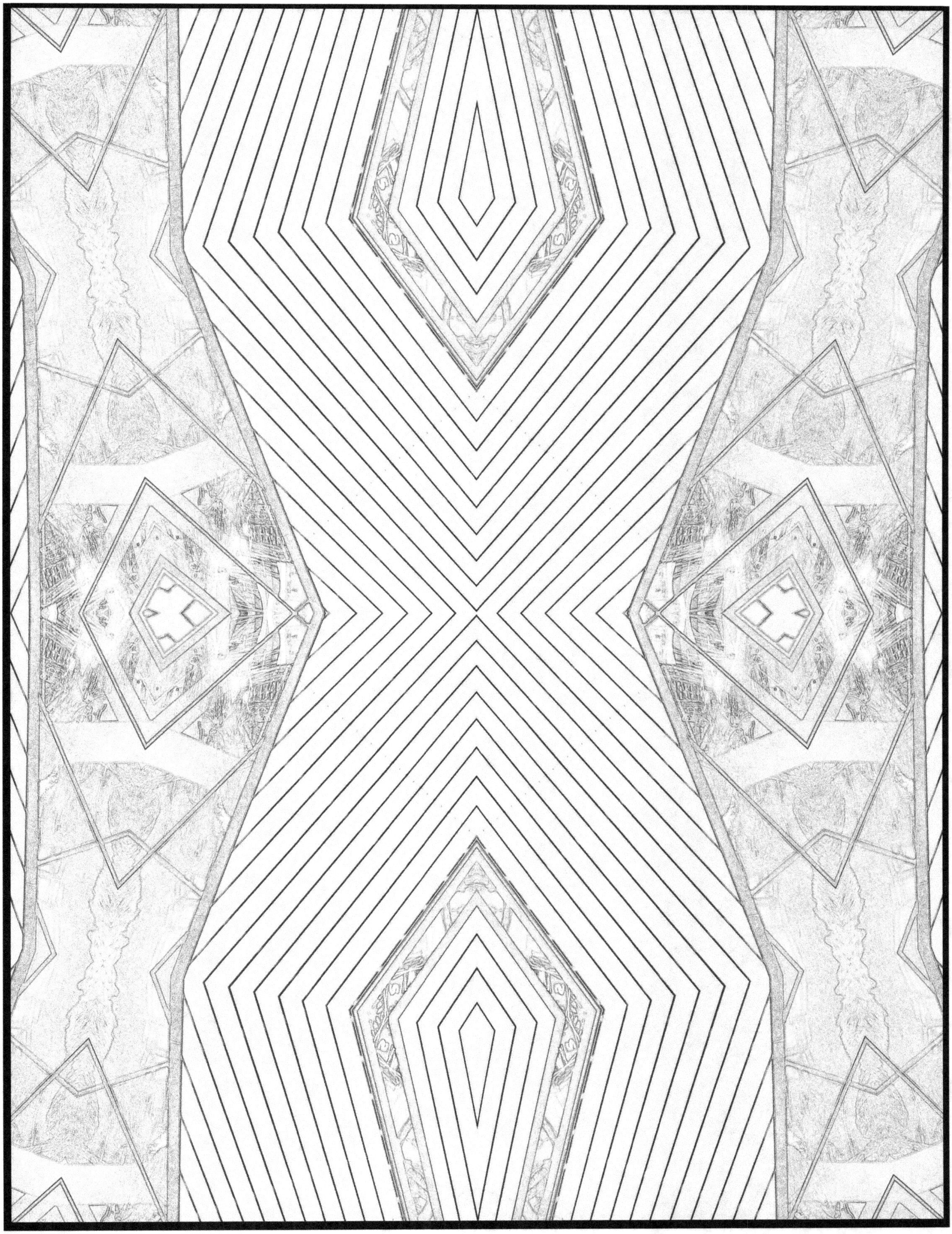

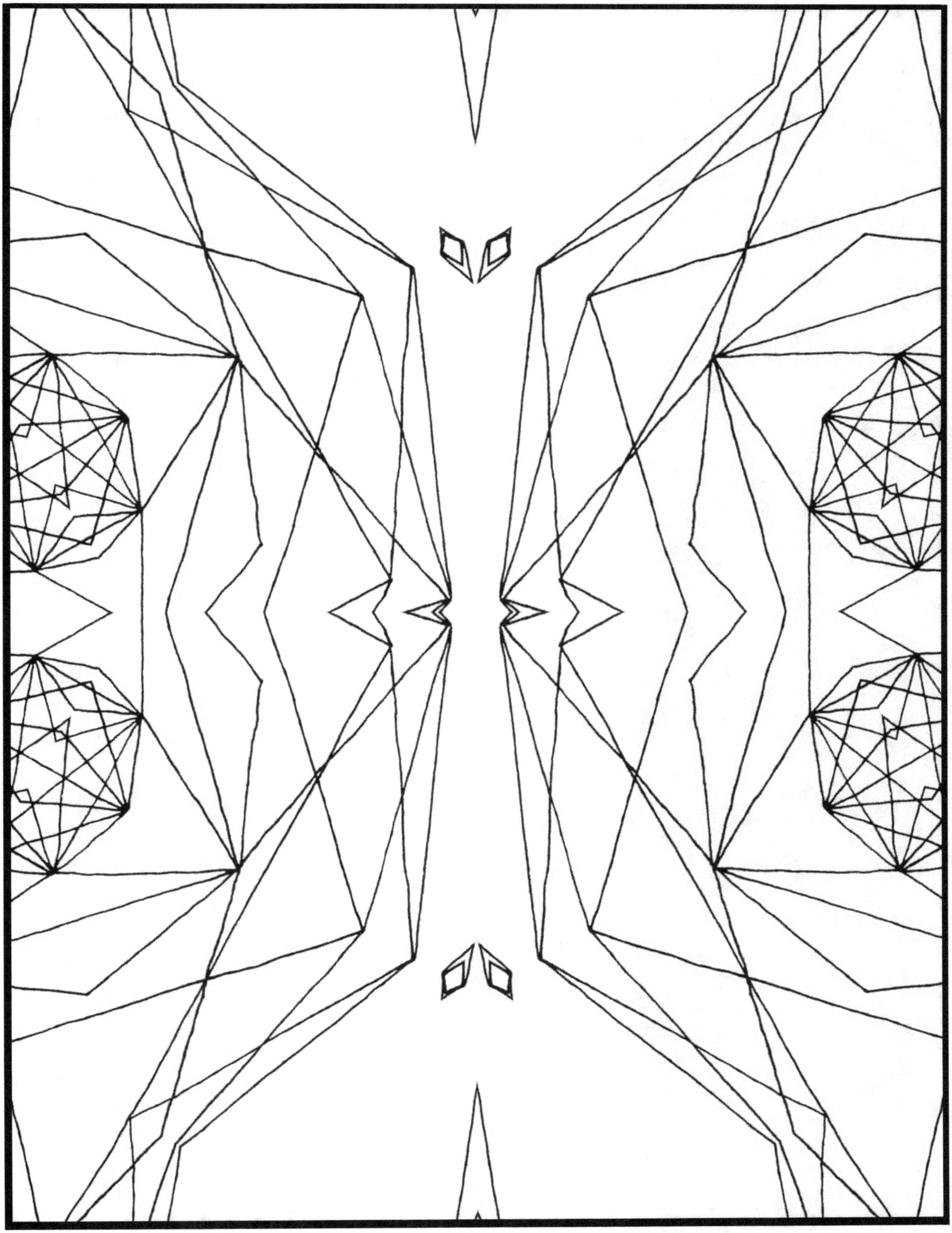

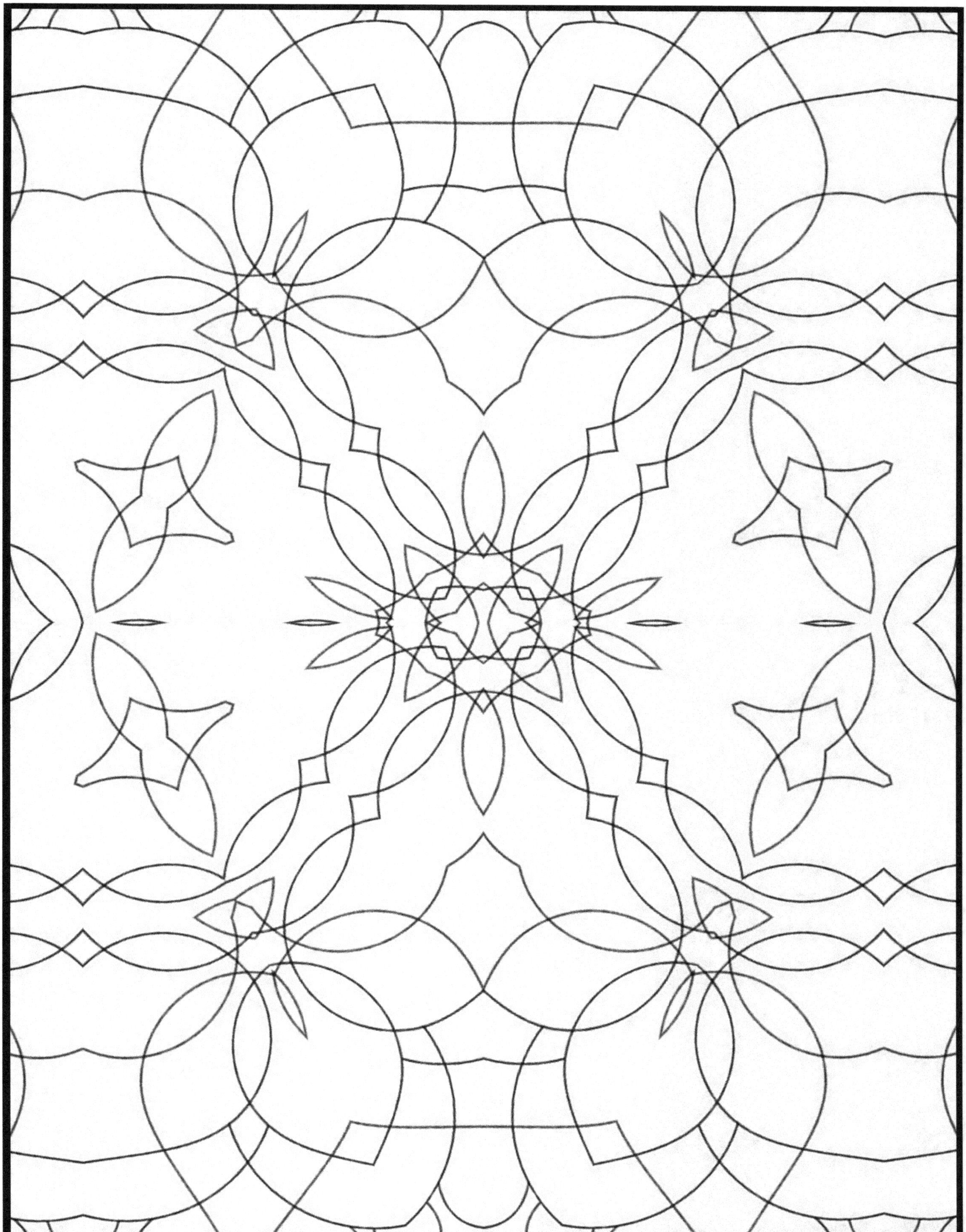

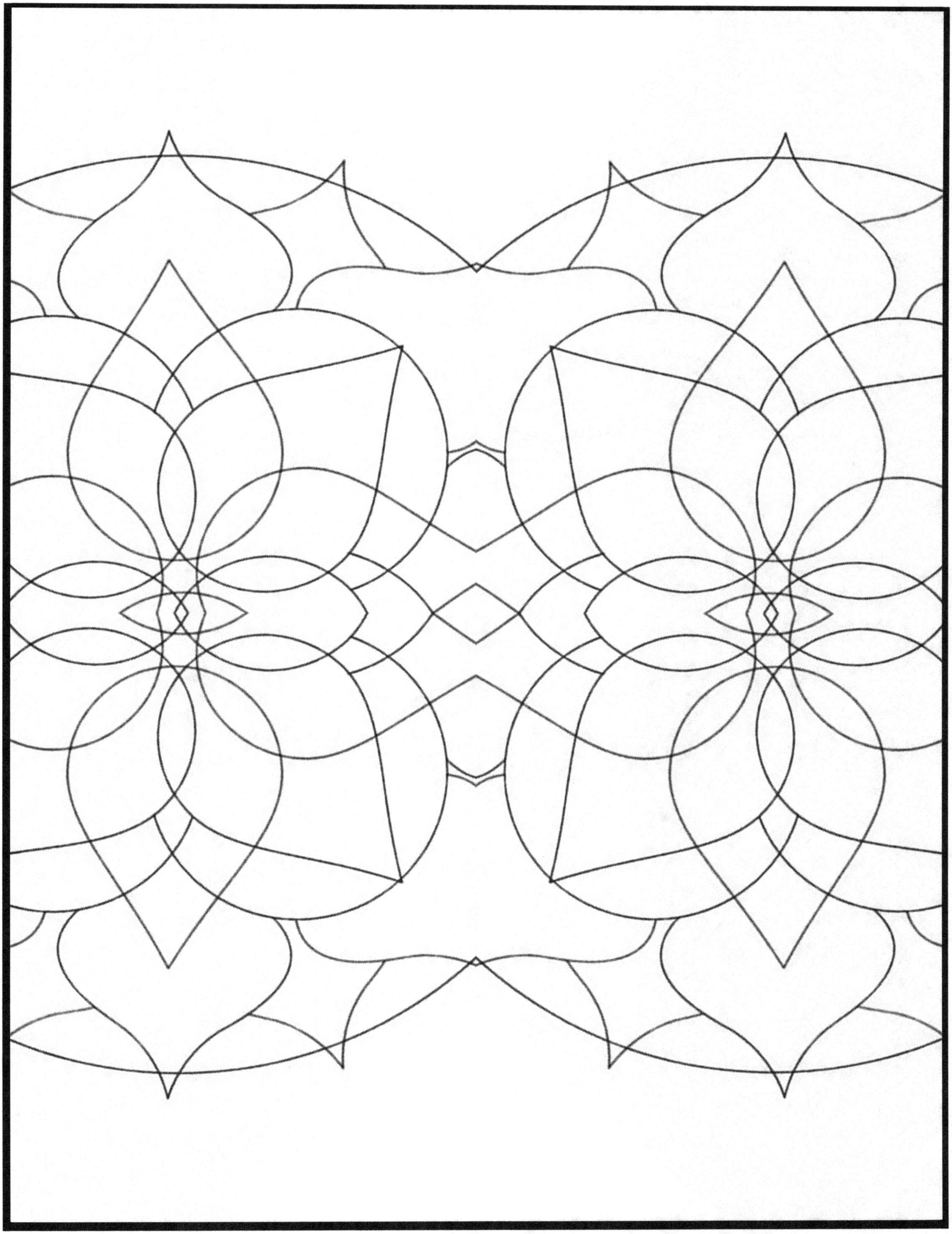

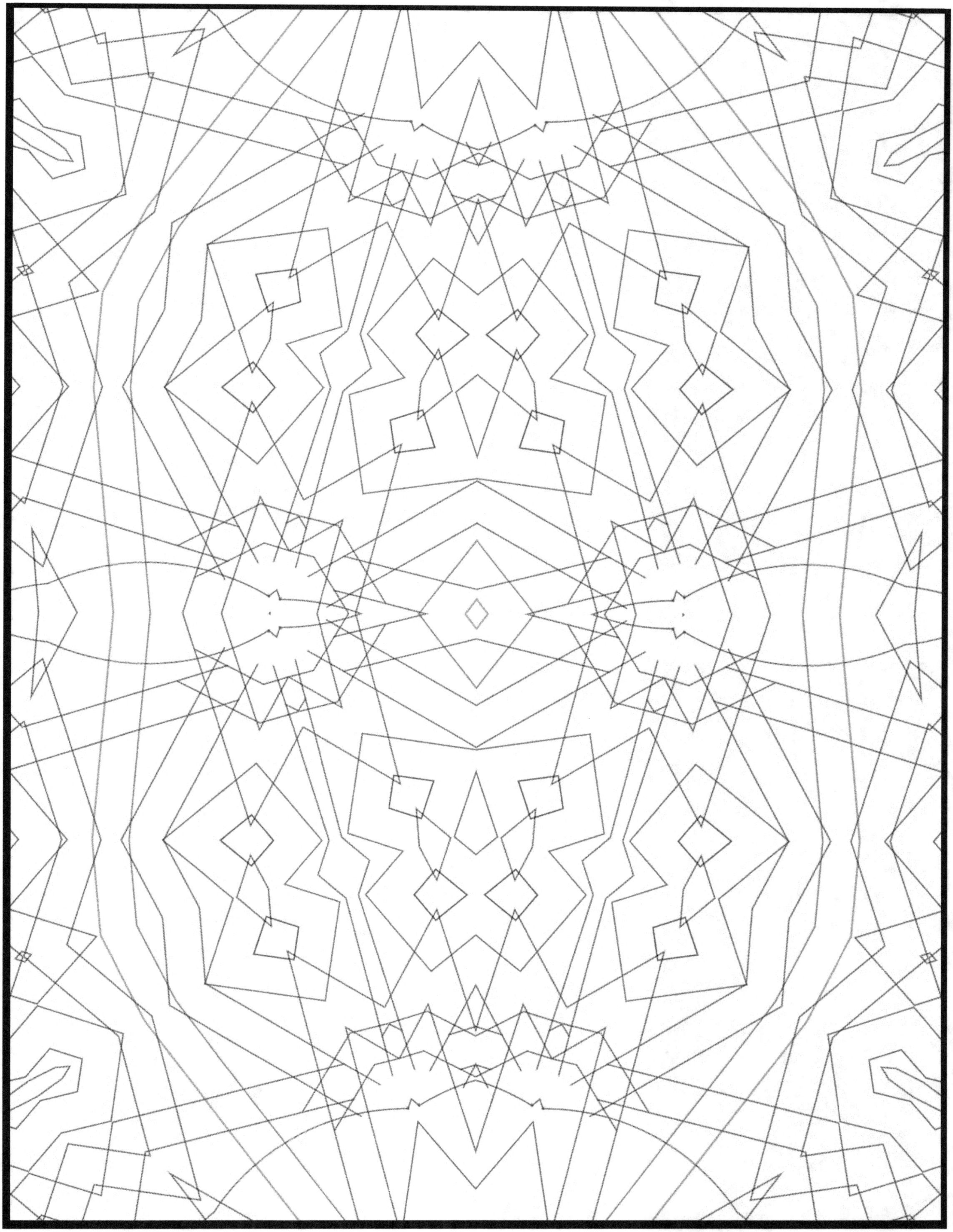

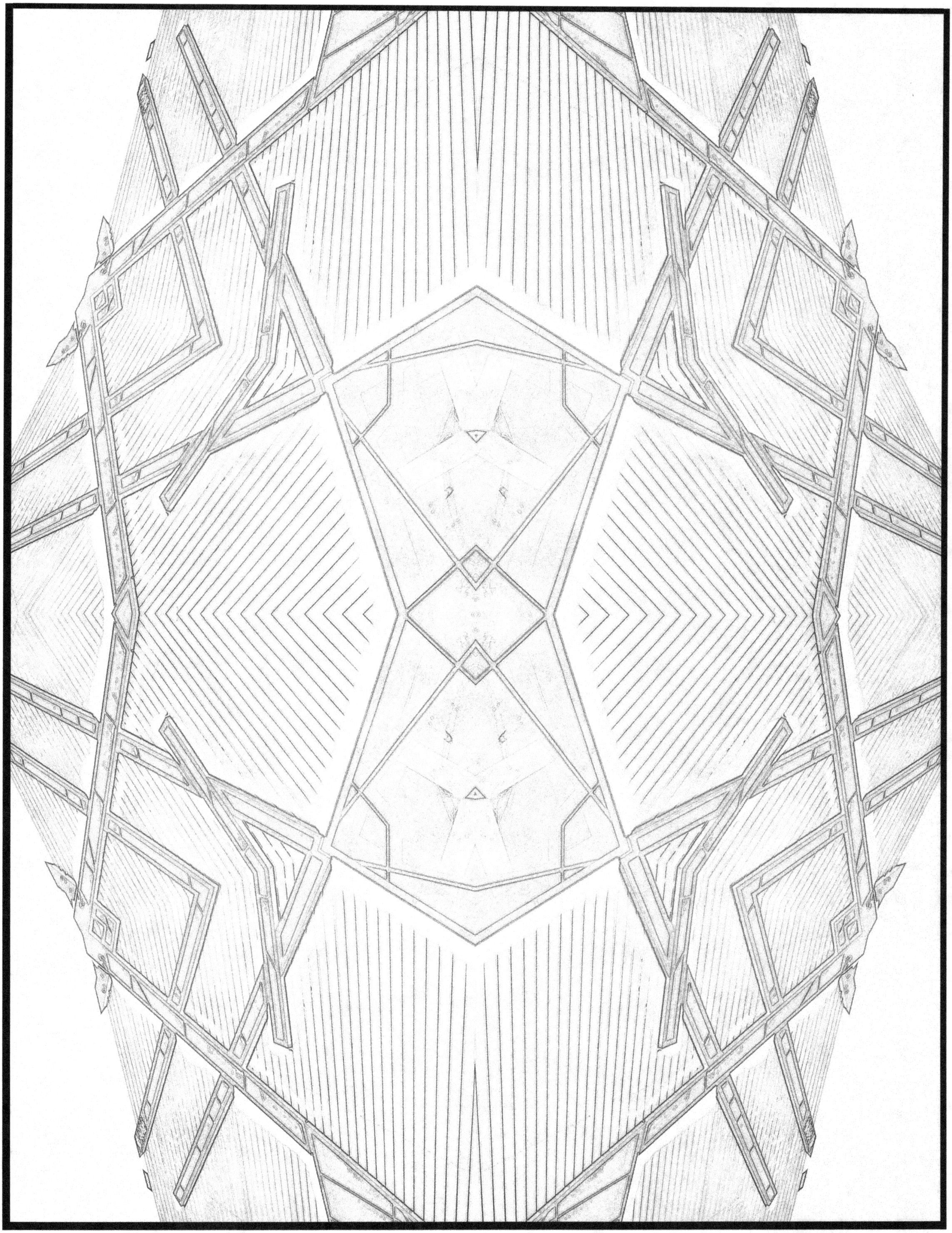

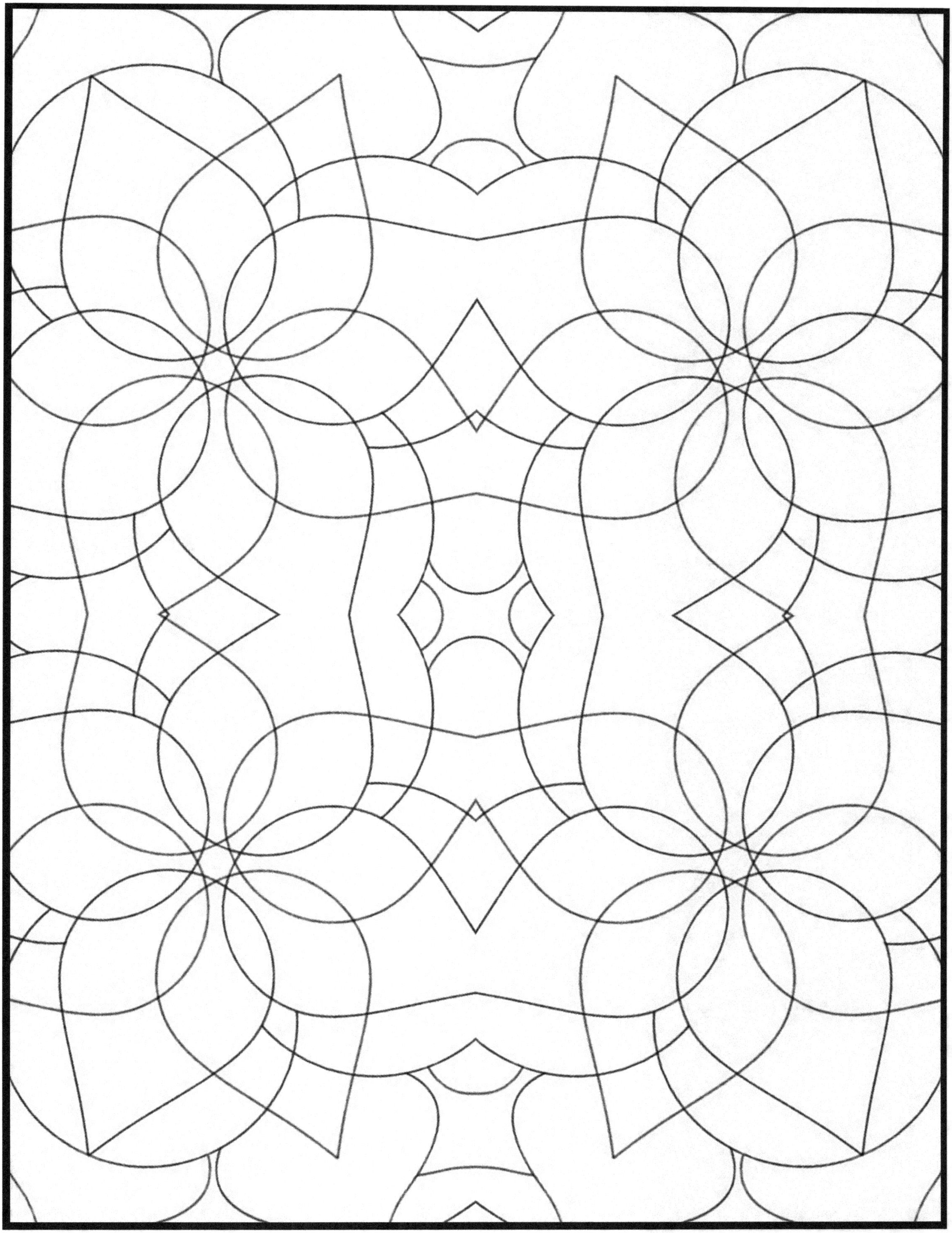

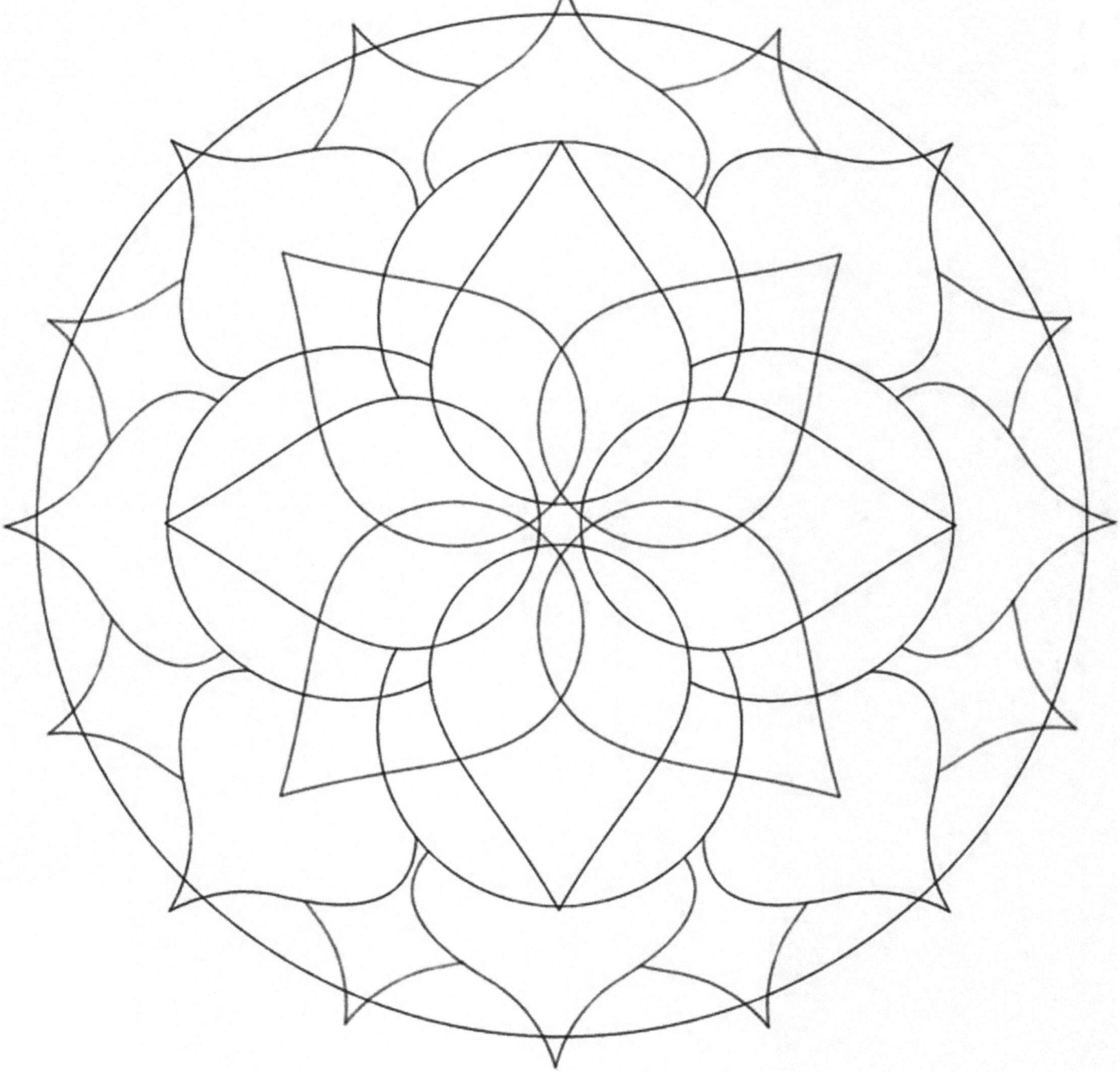

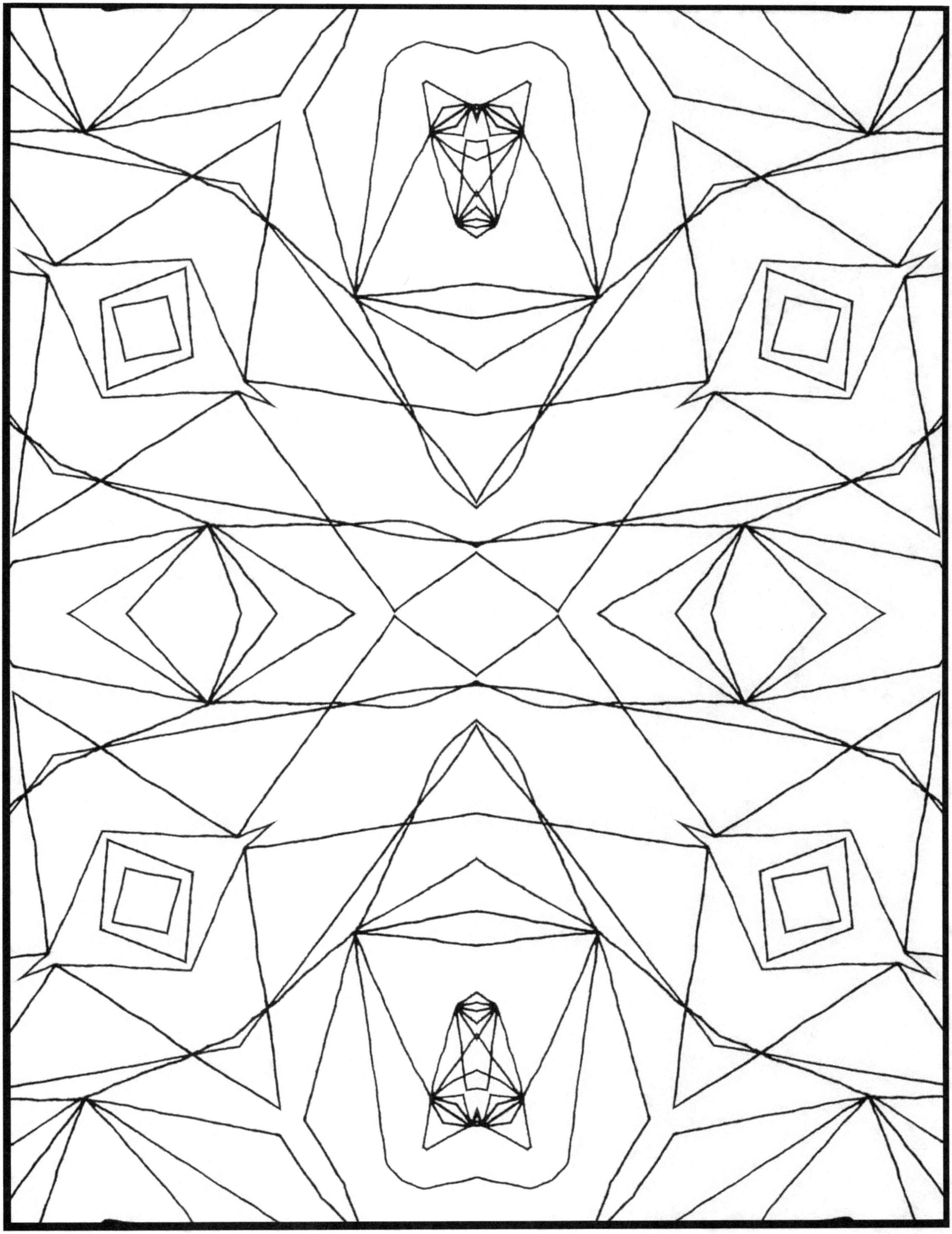

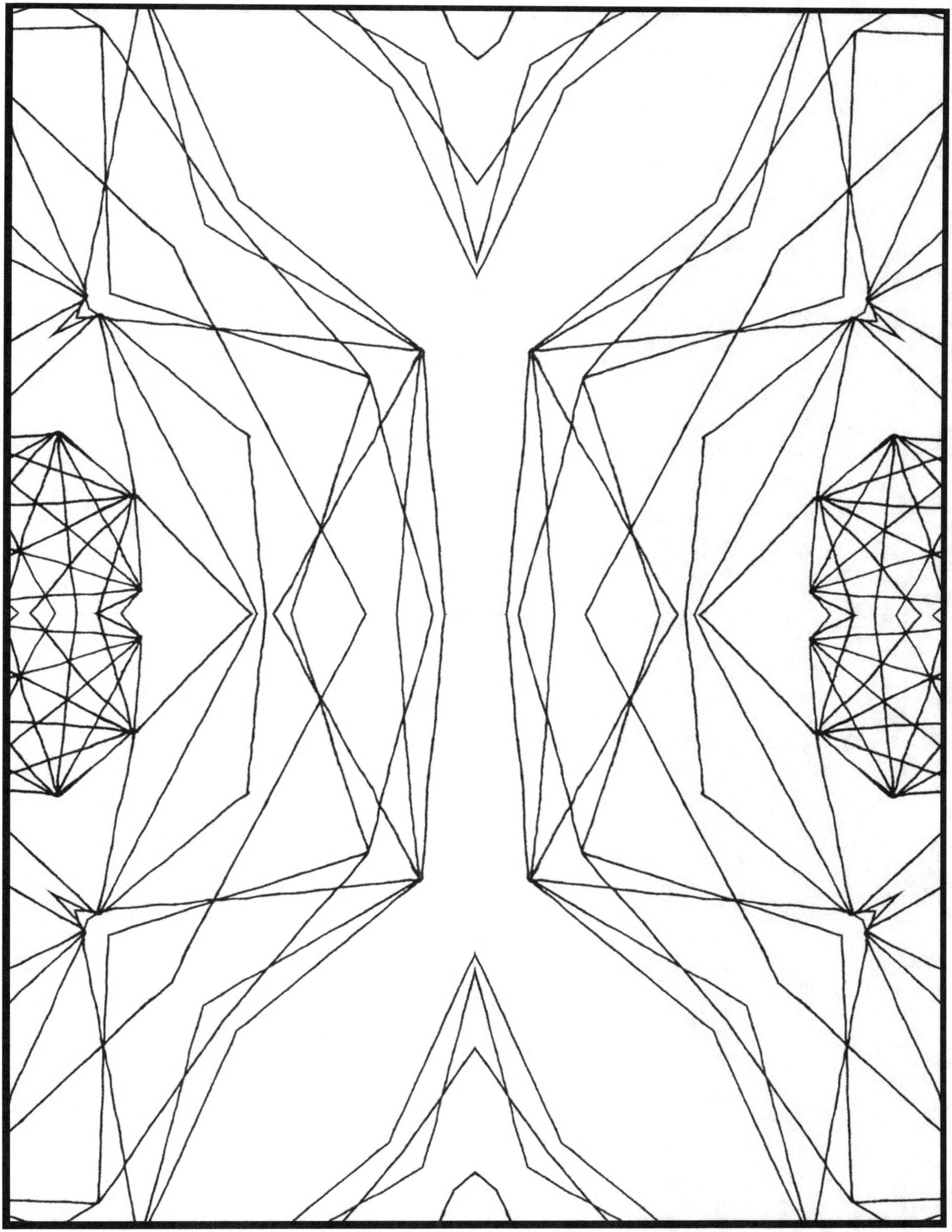

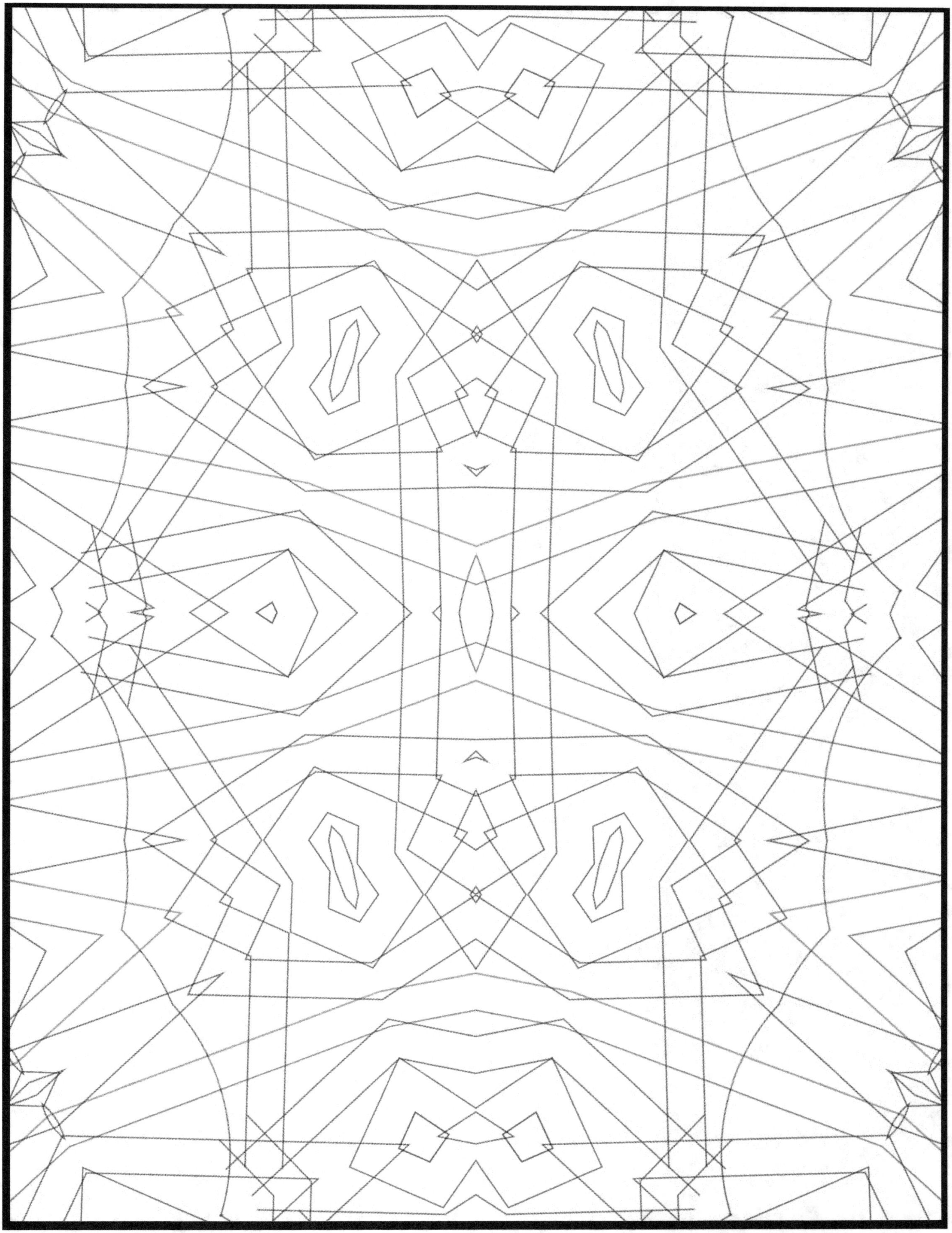

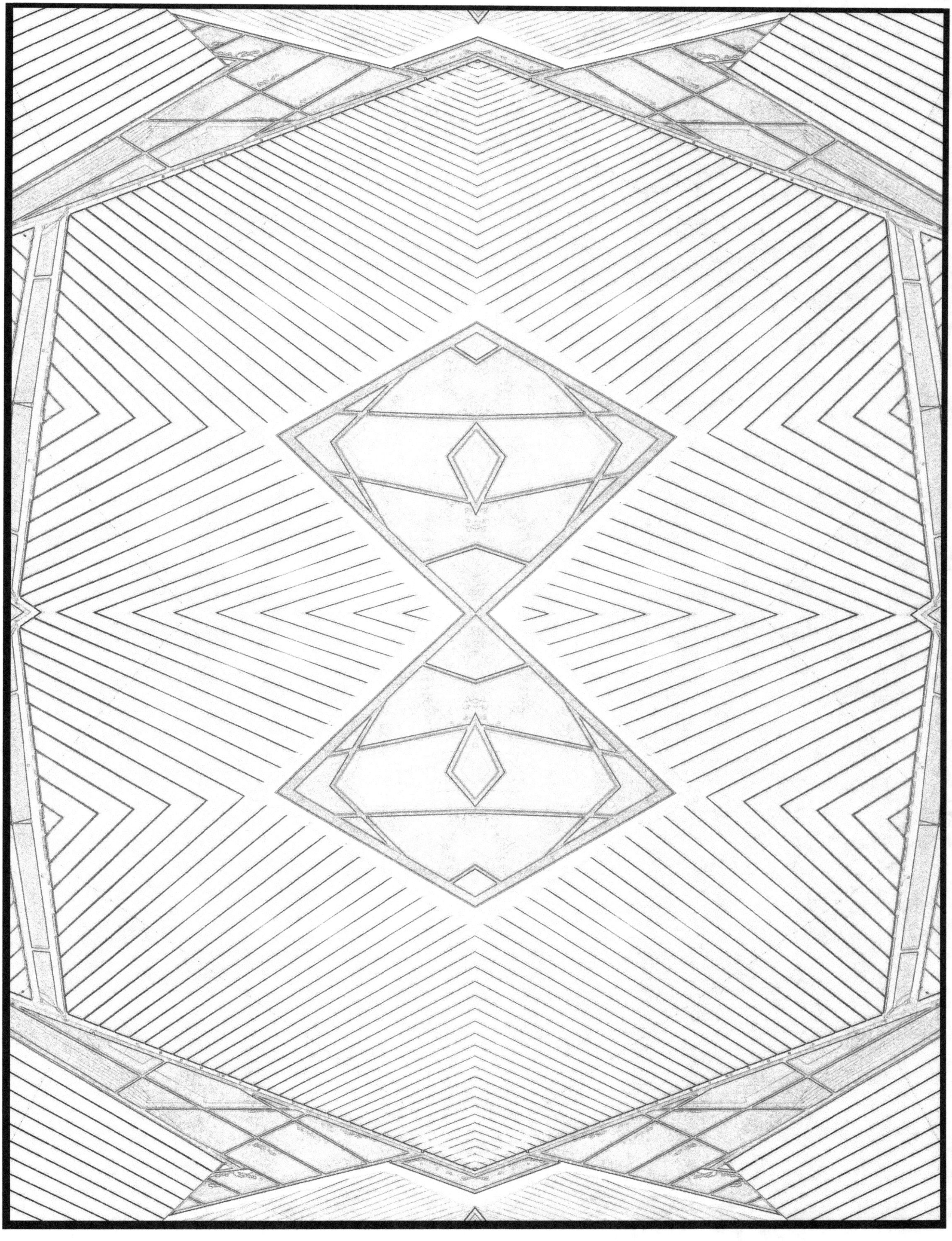

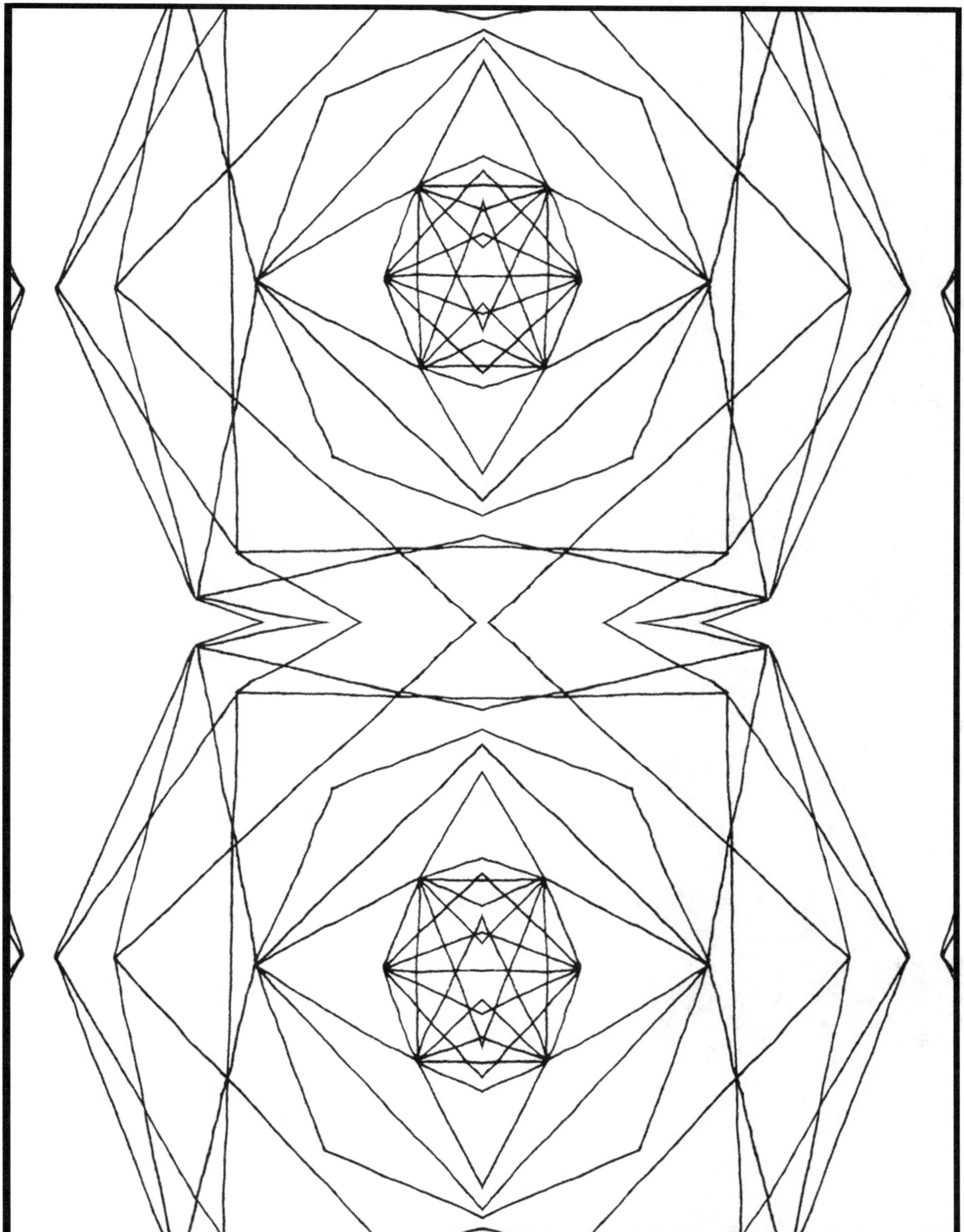

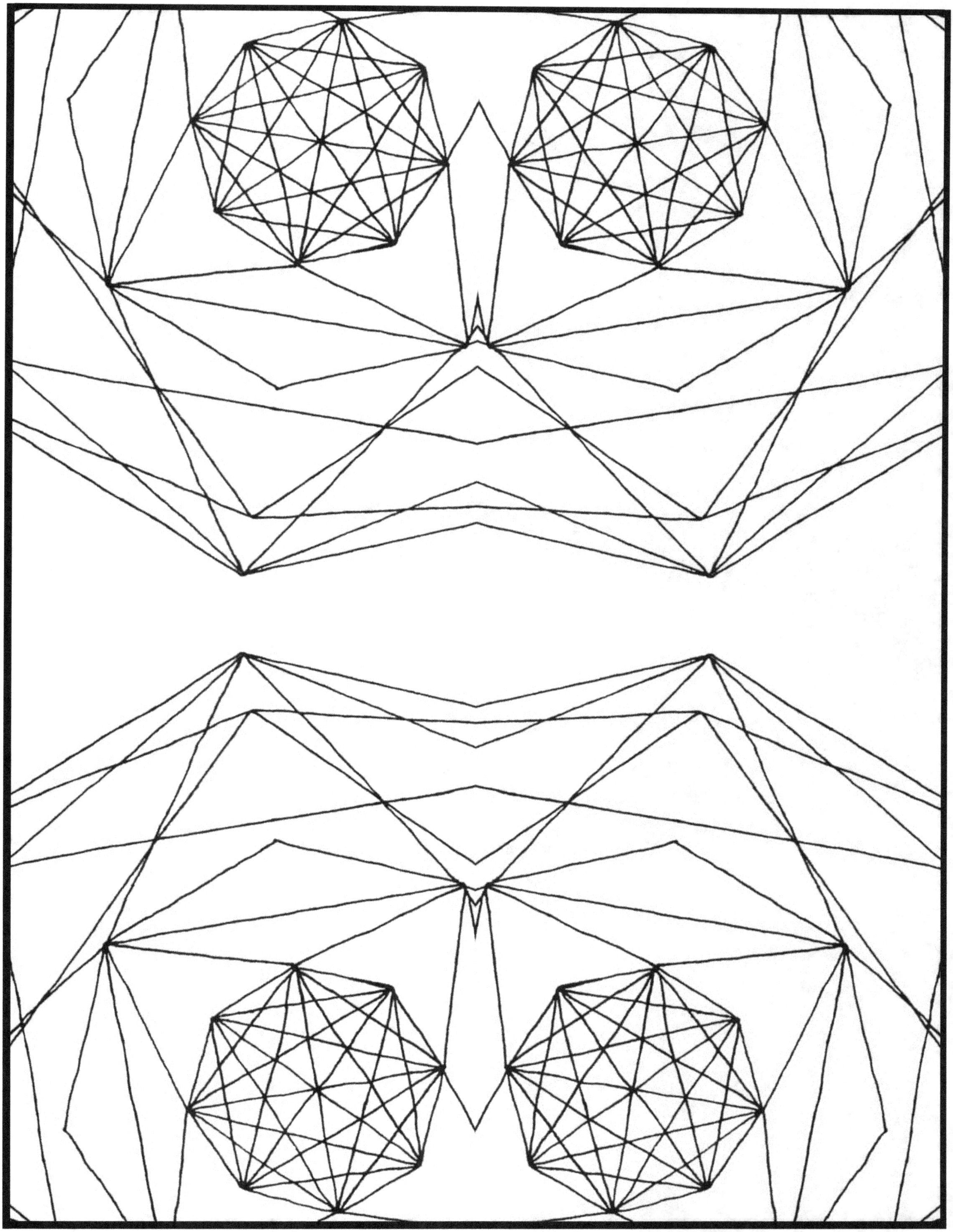

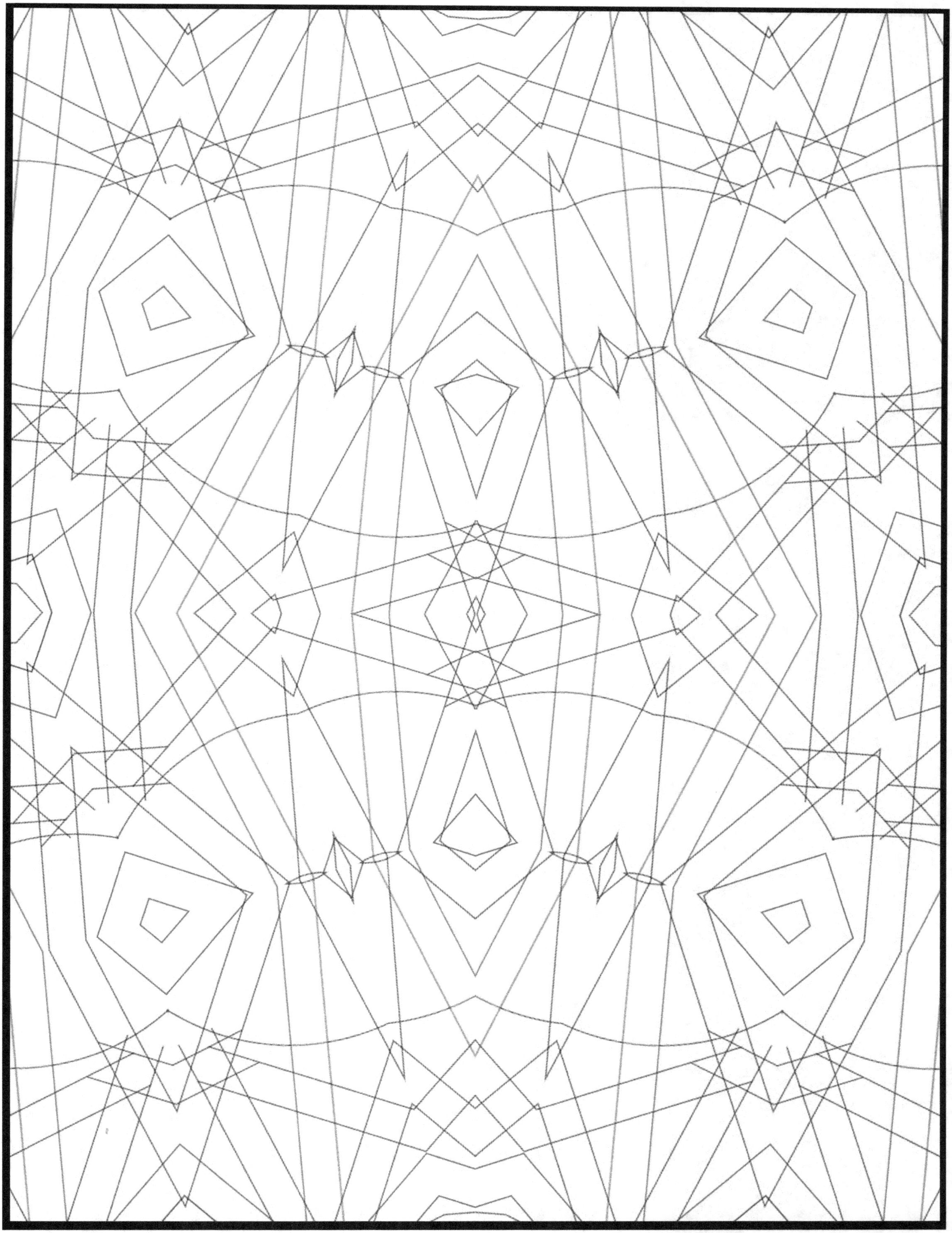

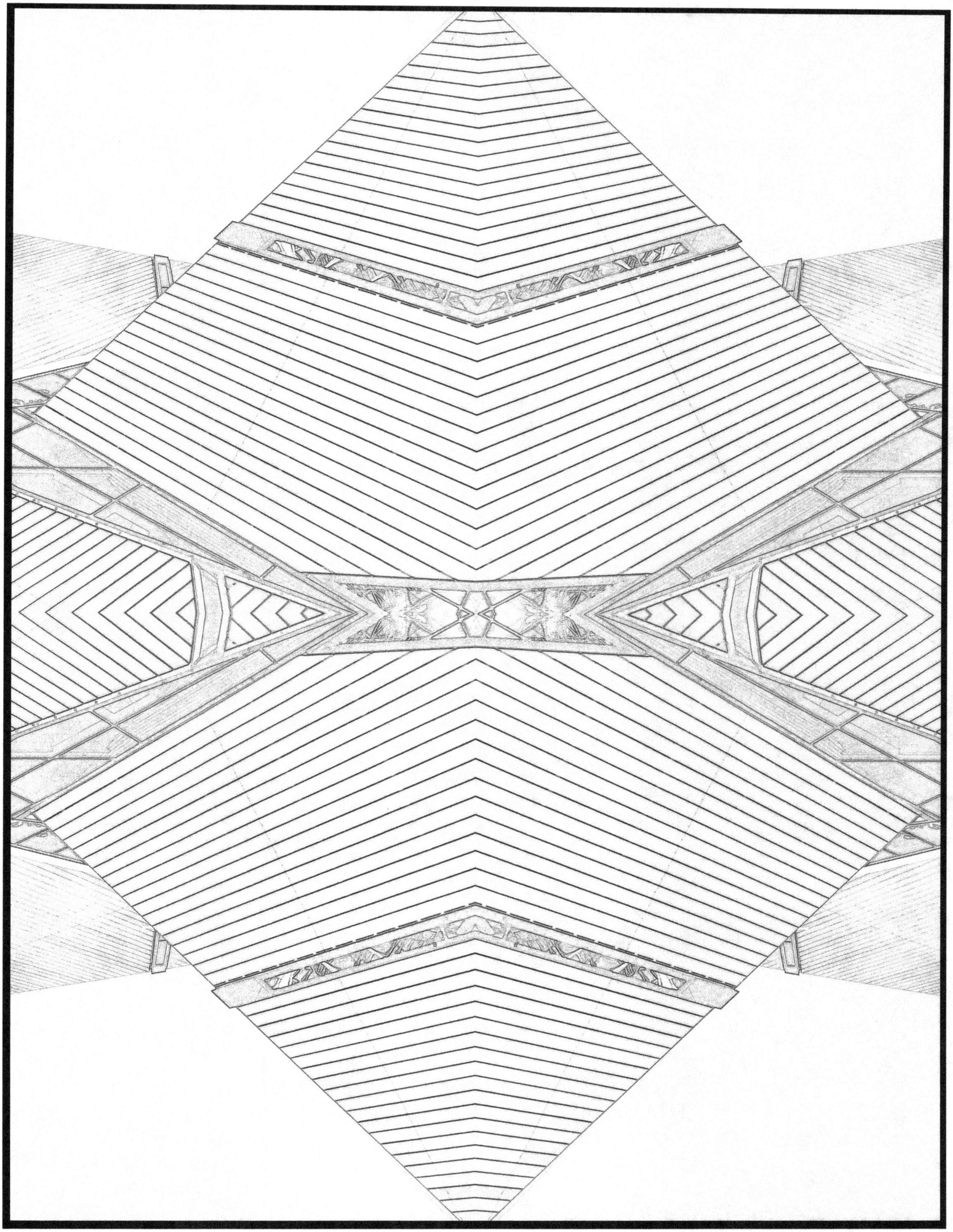

Thank you

**Hope you've enjoyed your coloring experience.
We here at ALENA will always strive to deliver
to you the highest quality coloring books.
So I'd like to thank you for supporting us.**

**Before you go, would you mind leaving us a review on Amazon?
It will mean a lot to us and support us creating
high quality guides for you in the future.**

**To get notificate for next new Coloring Books
Please follow our Amazon Author Page.**

**Warmly yours,
ALENA Team**

www.ingramcontent.com/pod-product-compliance
Lightning Source LLC
Chambersburg PA
CBHW081127180526
45170CB00008B/3039
* 9 7 8 1 5 4 2 7 2 5 2 0 0 *